WORLD'S GREATEST
STANDARDS

W9-BYK-704

51 of the Most Popular Standards Ever Written

This collection contains sheet music for some of the most enduring songs of all time, for unlimited hours of playing and singing pleasure. The world's greatest songwriters are represented, including Harold Arlen, Duke Ellington, George and Ira Gershwin®, Lorenz Hart, Johnny Mercer, Cole Porter, Richard Rodgers, Jule Styne, Harry Warren, and more.

In addition to dozens of long-established classics, you'll also find gems from recent decades, like "Killing Me Softly with His Song," "Moondance," "This Masquerade," "You Raise Me Up," and other hits that have deservedly established themselves as top-tier modern standards.

Alfred Publishing Co., Inc.
16320 Roscoe Blvd., Suite 100
P.O. Box 10003
Van Nuys, CA 91410-0003
alfred.com

ISBN-10: 0-7390-5688-3
ISBN-13: 978-0-7390-5688-2

Cover Photos
Clockwise from upper left: © istockphoto / b+ • © istockphoto / SL Photography • © Zoom-zoom / Dreamstime.com • © istockphoto / The-Tor

CONTENTS

AIN'T MISBEHAVIN'

Words by
ANDY RAZAF

Music by
THOMAS "FATS" WALLER and HARRY BROOKS

Ain't Misbehavin' - 5 - 1

6

8

are worth wait - in' for, be - lieve me.

I don't stay out late, don't care to go. I'm home a - bout eight, just

me and my ra - di - o. Ain't mis - be - hav - in', I'm sav - in' my love for

(Optional D.C. for 2nd Verse)

you.

you.

AT LAST

Lyrics by
MACK GORDON

Music by
HARRY WARREN

10

At Last - 3 - 2

AS TIME GOES BY

Words and Music by
HERMAN HUPFELD

Moderato, con espressione

This

day and age we're liv-ing in gives cause for ap-pre-hen-sion, with speed and new in-ven-tion, and

things like third di-men-sion. Yet, we get a tri-fle wea-ry, with Mis-ter Ein-stein's th-'ry. So we

As Time Goes By - 4 - 1

BEWITCHED, BOTHERED AND BEWILDERED

(from "Pal Joey")

Words by
LORENZ HART

Music by
RICHARD RODGERS

Bewitched, Bothered and Bewildered - 4 - 1

Moderately slow, with expression (♩ = 60)

Refrain:

since this half - pint im - i - ta - tion put me on the blink. I'm

wild a - gain! Be - guiled a - gain! A simp - er - ing, whimp - er - ing
Seen a lot; I mean a lot! But now I'm like sweet sev - en -

child a - gain. Be - witched, both - ered and be - wil - dered am
teen a lot. Be - witched, both - ered and be - wil - dered am

I._____
I._____
I'll sing to him and each
Could - n't sleep and

BLUE MOON

Lyrics by
LORENZ HART

Music by
RICHARD RODGERS

Calmly

Verse:

Once up-on a time, be - fore I took up smil - ing, I hat - ed the moon - light!
Once up-on a time my heart was just an or - gan, my life had no mis - sion.

Shad - ows of the night that po - ets find be - guil - ing seemed
Now that I have you, to be as rich as Mor - gan is

Blue Moon - 5 - 1

DREAM A LITTLE DREAM OF ME

Lyrics by
GUS KAHN

Music by
FABIAN ANDRE and WILBUR SCHWANDT

Dream a Little Dream of Me - 3 - 1

BLUES IN THE NIGHT
(My Mama Done Tol' Me)

Words by
JOHNNY MERCER

Music by
HAROLD ARLEN

BUT NOT FOR ME

featured in "Girl Crazy"

Music and Lyrics by
GEORGE GERSHWIN
and IRA GERSHWIN

Verse:

(pessimistically)

Old man sun - shine, lis - ten, you! Nev - er tell me, "Dreams come true!" Just

try it and I'll start a ri - ot.____

But Not for Me - 4 - 1

Rather slow *(smoothly)*

COME RAIN OR COME SHINE

Lyrics by
JOHNNY MERCER

Music by
HAROLD ARLEN

Come Rain or Come Shine - 4 - 1

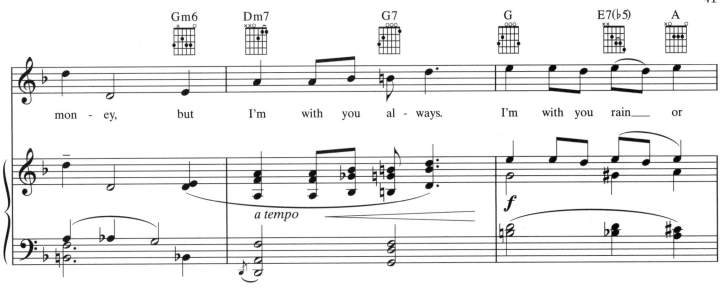

mon - ey, but I'm with you al - ways. I'm with you rain___ or

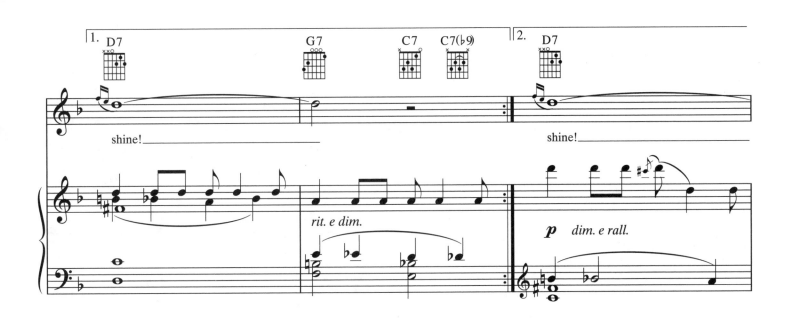

shine!_____ shine!_____

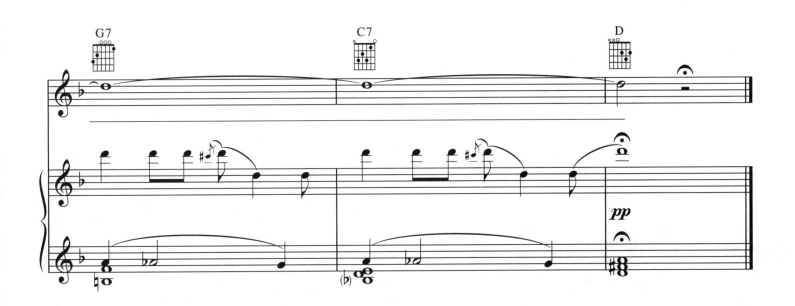

DON'T GET AROUND MUCH ANYMORE

Lyrics by
BOB RUSSELL

Music by
DUKE ELLINGTON

EMBRACEABLE YOU

Music and Lyrics by
GEORGE GERSHWIN
and IRA GERSHWIN

Male: Doz-ens of girls would storm up,
*Female: I went a-bout re-cit-ing,

I had to lock my door.
"Here's one who'll nev-er fall!"

Some-how I could-n't warm up to one be-fore.
But I'm a-fraid the writ-ing is on the wall.

* Alternate verse lyric.

Embraceable You - 4 - 1

EVERGREEN
(Love Theme from "A Star Is Born")

Words by
PAUL WILLIAMS

Music by
BARBRA STREISAND

Moderately, with feeling

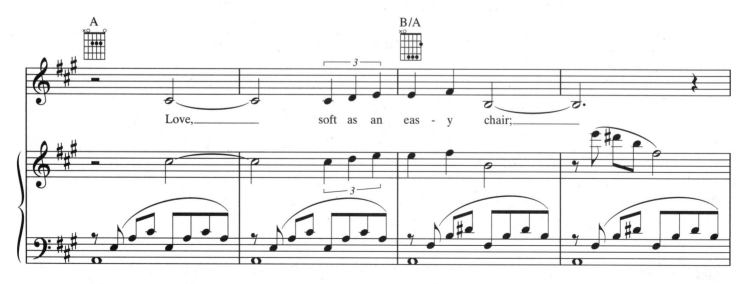

Evergreen - 6 - 1

FLY ME TO THE MOON
(In Other Words)

Words and Music by
BART HOWARD

FROM THIS MOMENT ON

Words and Music by
COLE PORTER

From This Moment On - 6 - 1

62

From This Moment On - 6 - 3

Lyrics:
on - ly ___ whoop - dee - doo songs,
from this mo - ment on. ___ For you've
got the love ___ I need so much, ___
Got the skin ___ I love to touch, ___

From This Moment On - 6 - 4

HOW DO I LIVE

Words and Music by
DIANE WARREN

70

with-out you?

Verse 2:
Without you, there'd be no sun in my sky,
There would be no love in my life,
There'd be no world left for me.
And I, baby, I don't know what I would do,
I'd be lost if I lost you.
If you ever leave,
Baby, you would take away everything real in my life.
And tell me now,
(To Chorus:)

From the Warner Bros. Motion Picture "BEST FRIENDS"

HOW DO YOU KEEP THE MUSIC PLAYING?

Lyrics by
ALAN and MARILYN BERGMAN

Music by
MICHEL LEGRAND

How do you keep the mu-sic play-ing? How do you make it last? How do you keep the song from fad-ing too fast?

How Do You Keep the Music Playing? - 5 - 1

HOW HIGH THE MOON

Lyrics by
NANCY HAMILTON

Music by
MORGAN LEWIS

I GET A KICK OUT OF YOU

(from "Anything Goes")

Words and Music by
COLE PORTER

IF EVER I WOULD LEAVE YOU

Lyrics by
ALAN JAY LERNER

Music by
FREDERICK LOEWE

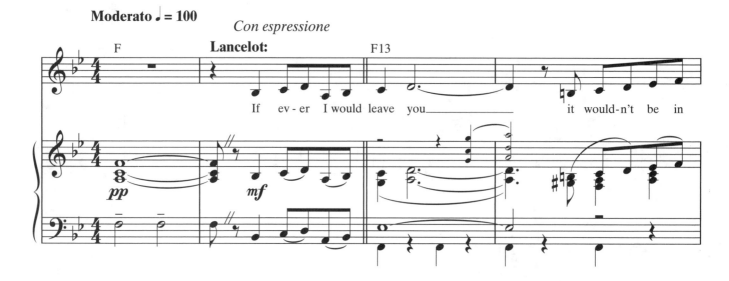

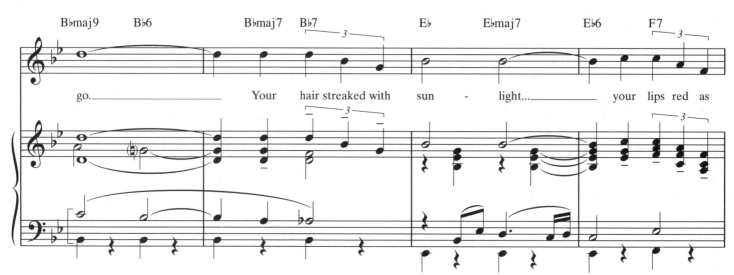

If Ever I Would Leave You - 4 - 1

If Ever I Would Leave You - 4 - 2

I'VE GOT A CRUSH ON YOU

Music and Lyrics by
GEORGE GERSHWIN
and IRA GERSHWIN

Allegretto giocoso

He: How
She: How

Verse:

glad the man-y mil-lions of An-na-belles and Lil-lians would be___
glad a mil-lion lad-ies from mil-lion-aires to cad-dies would be___

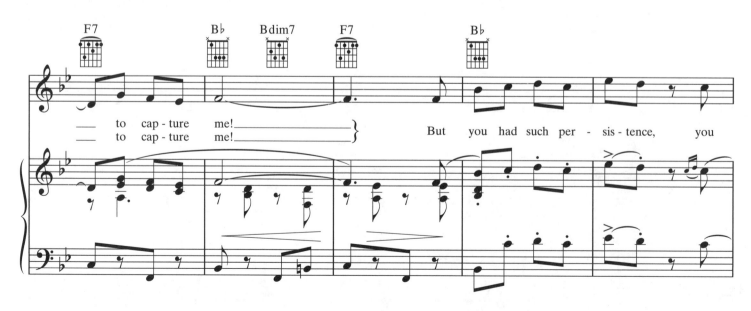

___ to cap-ture me!___
___ to cap-ture me!___

But you had such per-sis-tence, you

I've Got a Crush on You - 4 - 1

Moderately

I'VE GOT YOU UNDER MY SKIN

Words and Music by
COLE PORTER

JUST ONE OF THOSE THINGS

Words and Music by
COLE PORTER

Medium swing ♩ = 138

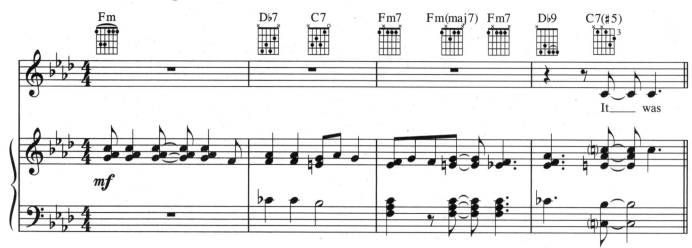

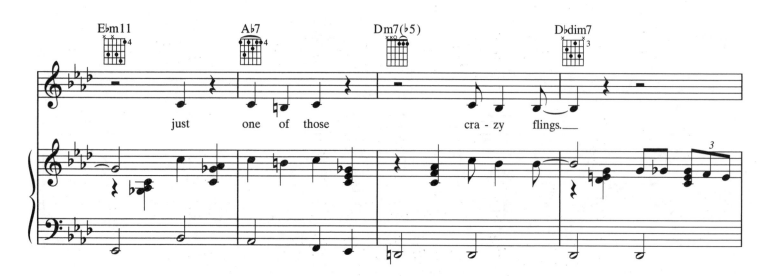

NIGHT AND DAY

(from "Gay Divorce")

Words and Music by
COLE PORTER

Night and Day - 5 - 5

KILLING ME SOFTLY WITH HIS SONG

Words and Music by
CHARLES FOX and NORMAN GIMBEL

Killing Me Softly With His Song - 6 - 3

112

LA VIE EN ROSE
(Take Me to Your Heart Again)

Original French Lyrics by EDITH PIAF
English Lyrics by MACK DAVID

Music by
LUIS GUGLIELMI

La Vie En Rose - 3 - 1

LAURA

Lyrics by
JOHNNY MERCER

Music by
DAVID RAKSIN

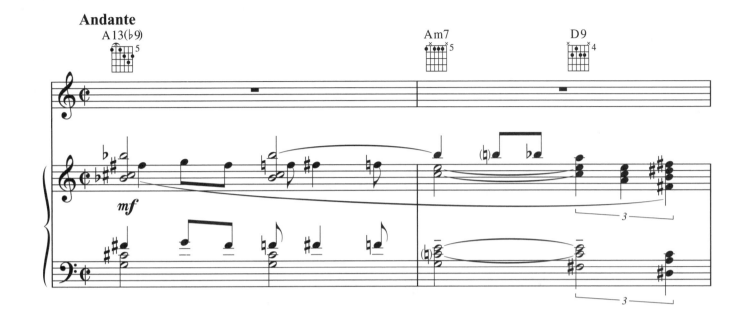

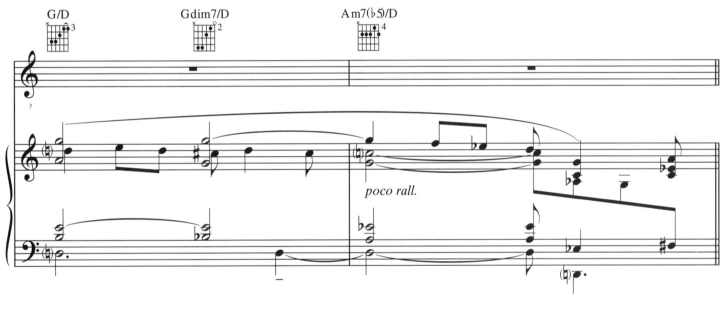

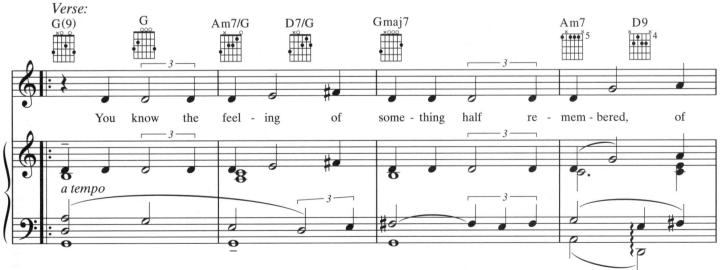

Laura - 5 - 1

Moderato

Chorus:

Lau - ra_____ is the face in the mist - y light,_____

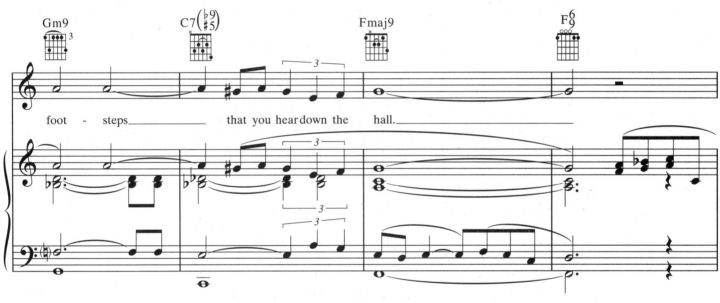

foot - steps_____ that you hear down the hall._____

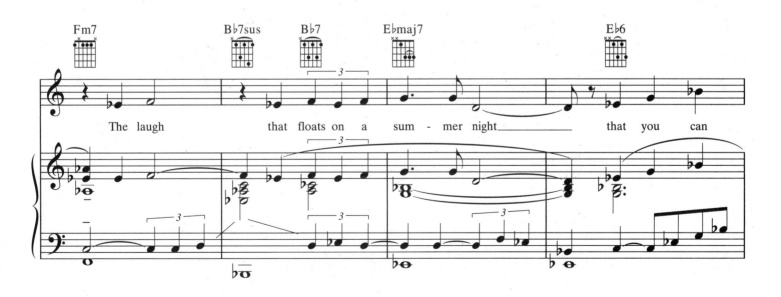

The laugh that floats on a sum - mer night_____ that you can

LEAVING ON A JET PLANE

Words and Music by
JOHN DENVER

125

Leaving on a Jet Plane - 4 - 4

MACK THE KNIFE

English Words by
MARC BLITZSTEIN
Original German Words by
BERT BRECHT

Music by
KURT WEILL

MAKIN' WHOOPEE!

Words by
GUS KAHN

Music by
WALTER DONALDSON

MISTY

Words by
JOHNNY BURKE

Music by
ERROLL GARNER

thou-sand vi - o - lins be - gin to play,

mu - sic I hear._____ I get mist - y the mo - ment you're near.

You can say that you're lead - ing me on,_____ but it's just what I

want you to do._____ Don't you no - tice how hope - less - ly I'm lost?_____

MOONDANCE

Words and Music by
VAN MORRISON

MY FUNNY VALENTINE

Words by
LORENZ HART

Music by
RICHARD RODGERS

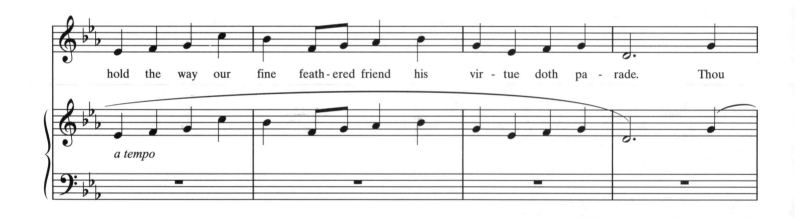

hold the way our fine feath-ered friend his vir-tue doth pa-rade. Thou

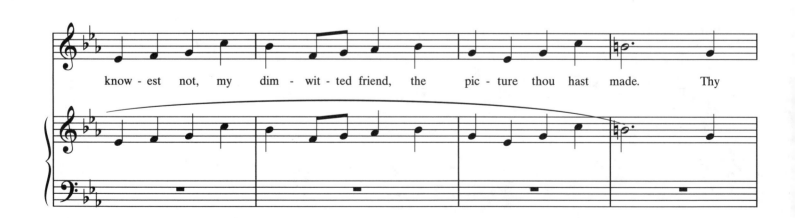

know-est not, my dim-wit-ted friend, the pic-ture thou hast made. Thy

from "ON A CLEAR DAY YOU CAN SEE FOREVER"

ON A CLEAR DAY
(You Can See Forever)

Words by
ALAN JAY LERNER

Music by
BURTON LANE

On a Clear Day (You Can See Forever) - 4 - 4

ON THE STREET WHERE YOU LIVE

Words by
ALAN JAY LERNER

Music by
FREDERICK LOEWE

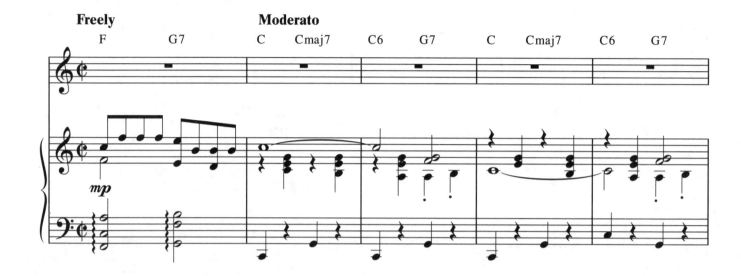

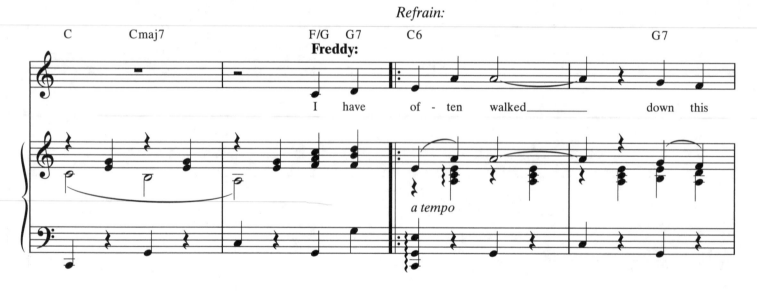

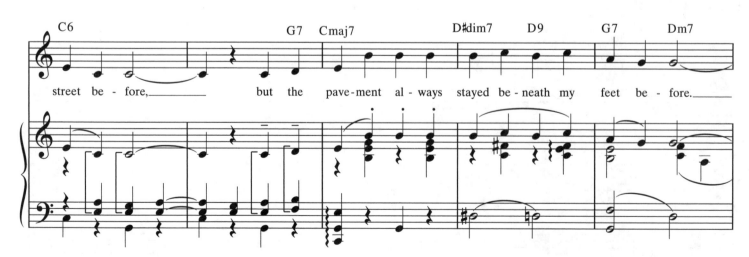

On the Street Where You Live - 4 - 1

153

On the Street Where You Live - 4 - 2

Featured in the MGM Picture "THE WIZARD OF OZ"

OVER THE RAINBOW

Lyric by
E.Y. HARBURG

Music by
HAROLD ARLEN

Over the Rainbow - 4 - 1

Some - where o - ver the rain - bow blue - birds fly.

Birds fly o - ver the rain - bow, why then, oh why can't I?

I? If

hap - py lit - tle blue-birds fly be - yond the rain - bow, why oh why can't I?

PEOPLE
(from "Funny Girl")

Words by
BOB MERRILL

Music by
JULE STYNE

Moderately

Verse:

People,_____ peo - ple who need peo - ple_____ are the

luck - i - est peo - ple_____ in the world._____ We're chil - dren

espressivo

need - ing oth - er chil - dren,_____ and yet, let - ting our grown - up

People - 3 - 1

deep in your soul_____ says, "You were half, now you're whole."_____ No more

hun - ger and thirst, but first, be a per - son who needs peo - ple._____ Peo - ple who need

peo - ple_____ are the luck - i - est peo - ple in the

world._____ world._____

SATIN DOLL

Words and Music by
JOHNNY MERCER, DUKE ELLINGTON
and BILLY STRAYHORN

THE SHADOW OF YOUR SMILE

Lyrics by
PAUL FRANCIS WEBSTER

Music by
JOHNNY MANDEL

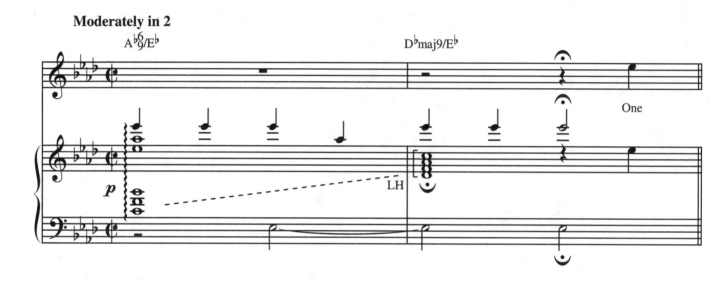

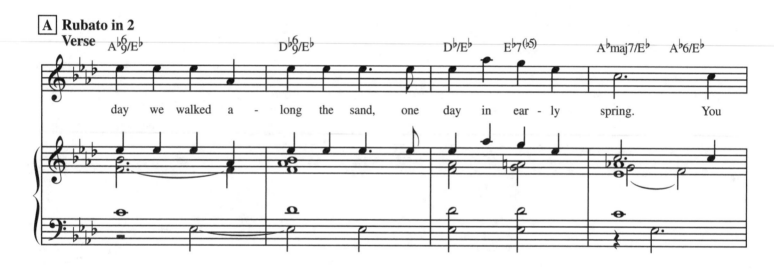

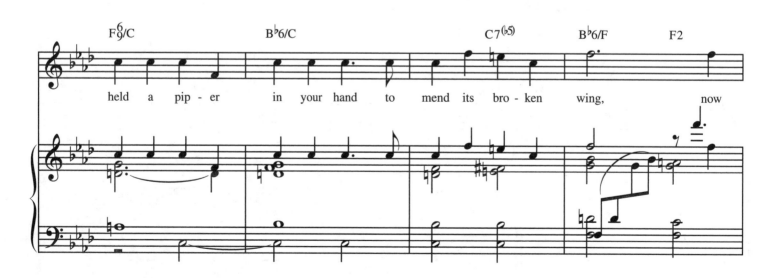

The Shadow of Your Smile - 4 - 1

SINGIN' IN THE RAIN

featured in "Hollywood Revue of 1929" and "Singin' in the Rain"

Lyric by
ARTHUR FREED

Music by
NACIO HERB BROWN

To Coda ⊕

SOMEONE TO WATCH OVER ME

Music and Lyrics by
GEORGE GERSHWIN
and IRA GERSHWIN

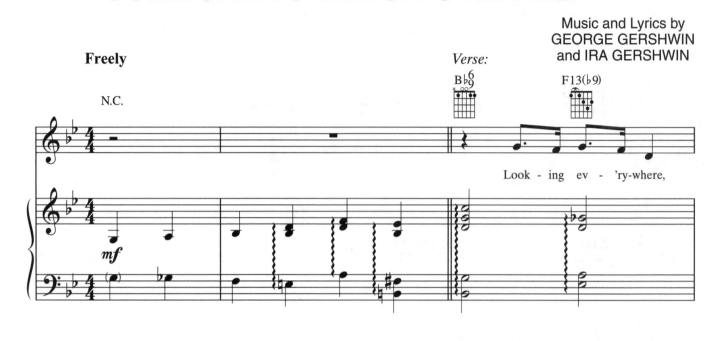

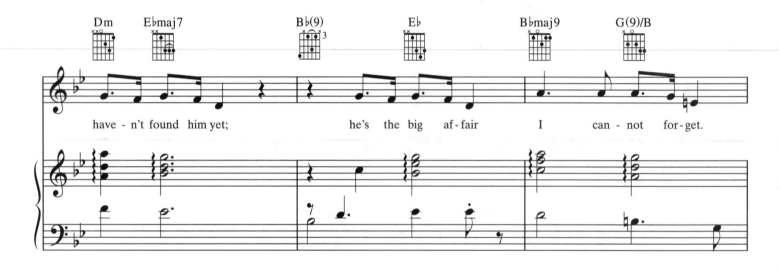

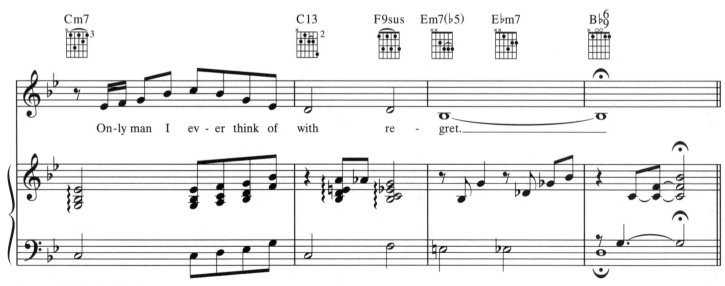

Someone to Watch Over Me - 4 - 1

STAR DUST

Words by
MITCHELL PARISH

Music by
HOAGY CARMICHAEL

Star Dust - 4 - 1

180

love was new, and each kiss an in-spir-a - tion._____ But
mour fût jeune, et chaque bai - ser in-spir-a - tion._____ Lei

that was long a - go; now my con-so-la - tion is in the star dust of a
ann - ées sont pa - ssées et ma con-so-la - tion s'é leve à t'é - toile d'une chan-

song. Be - side a gar - den wall, when stars are bright,
son. É - toile du soir brill - ant é - toille d'a - mour

you are in my arms. The night-in - gale tells his fair - y tale
tu es dans mes bras. Le ros - si - gnole chante et puis à'en vole

of par - a - dise where ros - es grew._____ Though I dream in vain,_____ in my
au pa - ra - dis des âmes ra - vies._____ Done mon rêve a'en - fuit._____ Comme une

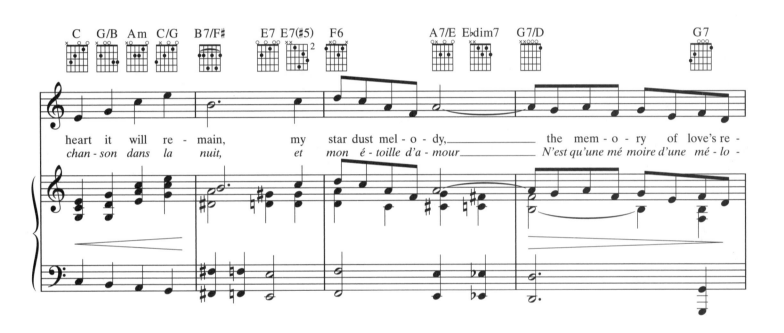

heart it will re - main, my star dust mel - o - dy,_____ the mem - o - ry of love's re -
chan - son dans la nuit, et mon é - toille d'a - mour_____ N'est qu'une mé moire d'une mé - lo -

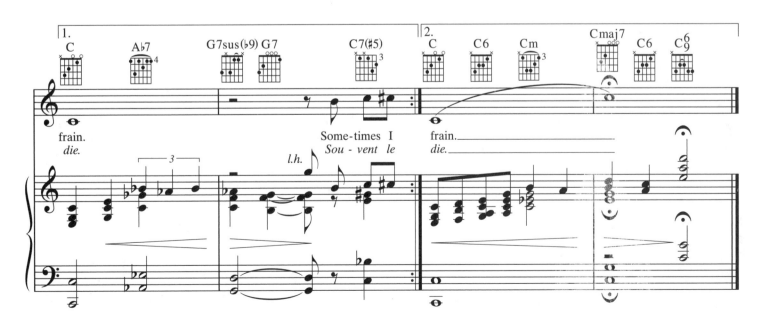

frain. Some-times I frain._____
die. Sou - vent le die._____

SUMMER WIND

English Words by JOHNNY MERCER
Original German Lyrics by HANS BRADTKE

Music by
HENRY MAYER

Summer Wind - 6 - 1

185

Summer Wind - 6 - 4

SUMMERTIME

Music and Lyrics by
GEORGE GERSHWIN, IRA GERSHWIN
and DuBOSE and DOROTHY HEYWARD

Allegretto semplice

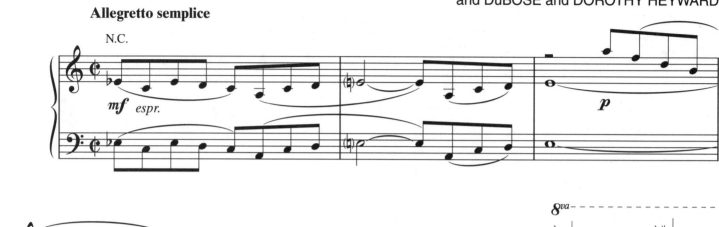

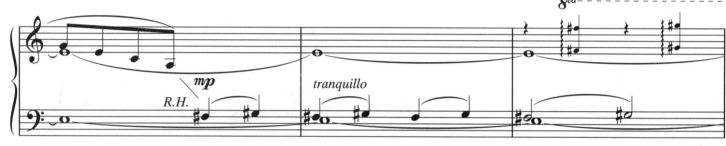

Moderately, with expression ($\quad$ = 40)

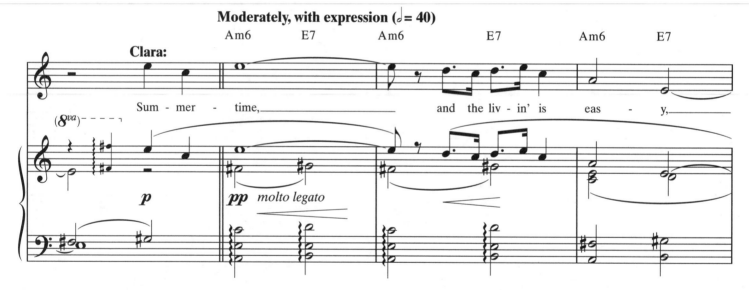

Sum - mer - time,_____ and the liv - in' is eas - y,_____

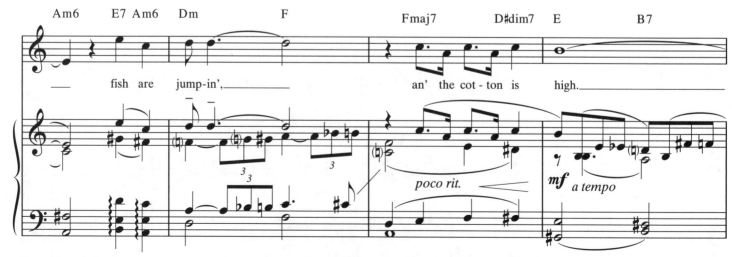

____ fish are jump-in',_____ an' the cot - ton is high._____

Summertime - 3 - 1

From the Columbia Picture "REVEILLE WITH BEVERLY"

TAKE THE "A" TRAIN

Words and Music by
BILLY STRAYHORN

Refrain:

THEME FROM NEW YORK, NEW YORK

Words by
FRED EBB

Music by
JOHN KANDER

Theme From New York, New York - 5 - 1

Verse 2:

Bridge 2:

THIS MASQUERADE

Words and Music by
LEON RUSSELL

(Scat vocal and Guitar)

(Scat vocal and Guitar continue ad lib.)

This Masquerade - 5 - 1

Repeat ad lib. and fade

TRY TO REMEMBER

(from "The Fantasticks")

Lyrics by
TOM JONES

Music by
HARVEY SCHMIDT

Slowly, with tenderness (in one)

Try to re - mem - ber the kind of Sep - tem - ber when
Try to re - mem - ber when life was so ten - der that

life was slow and oh, so mel - low.___
no one wept ex - cept the wil - low.___

Try to Remember - 3 - 1

WHEN I FALL IN LOVE

Words by
EDWARD HEYMAN

Music by
VICTOR YOUNG

Slowly, with much feeling ♩ = 84

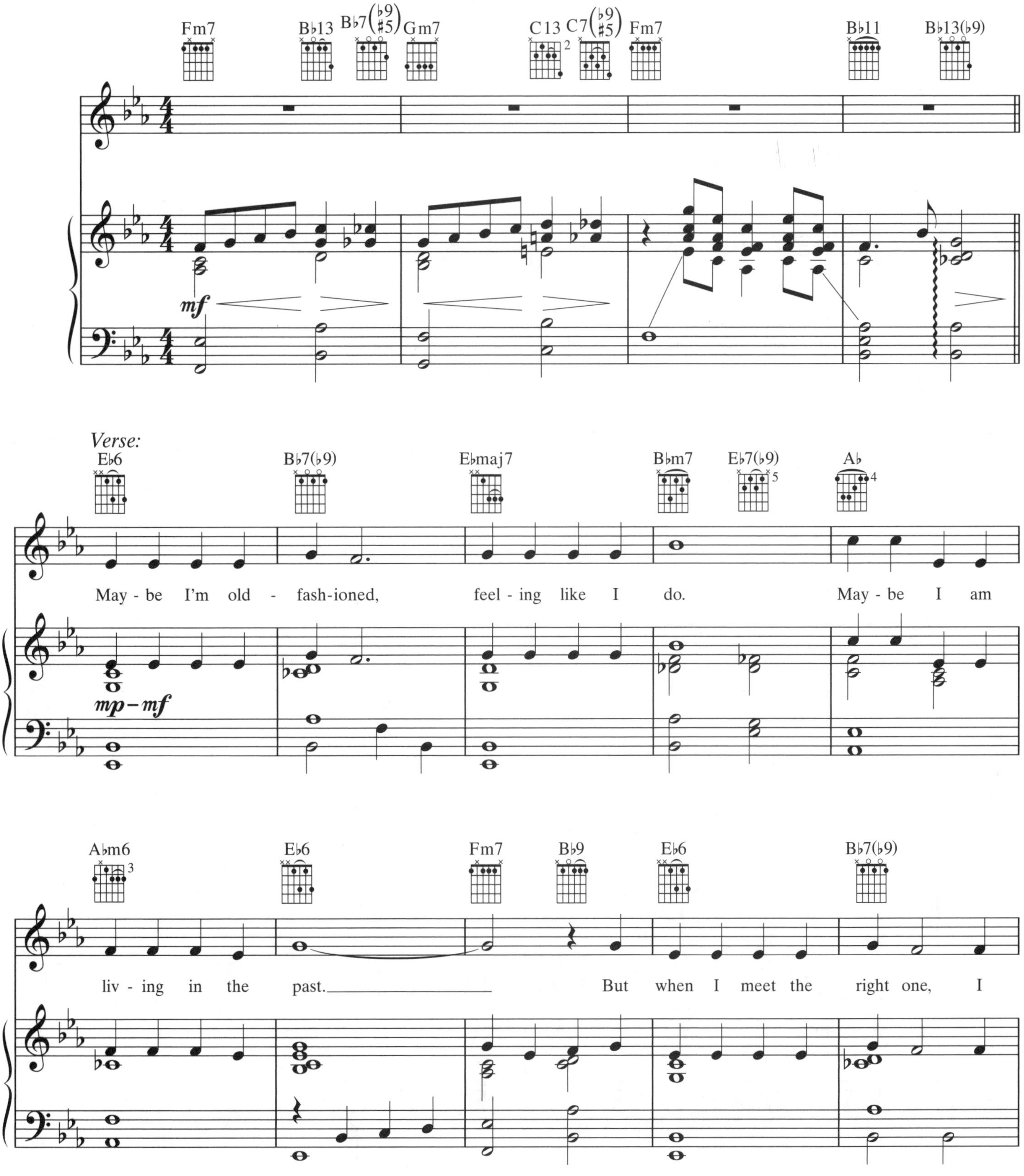

208

When I Fall in Love - 3 - 2

WHAT A WONDERFUL WORLD

Words and Music by
GEORGE DAVID WEISS and BOB THIELE

WHERE OR WHEN

(from "Babes In Arms")

Words by
LORENZ HART

Music by
RICHARD RODGERS

Refrain: (with much sentiment)

216

YOU RAISE ME UP

Words and Music by
ROLF LOVLAND and
BRENDAN GRAHAM

Freely, with expression

(with pedal)

Verse:

down   and oh,   my soul, so wea-ry,_____   when trou-bles   come   and my heart bur-dened

You Raise Me Up - 5 - 1